Finding the Right Direction for Success in Life

<•••)•(•••>

A Country Boy's Story

A. Patten, Jr.

Fulton Books
Meadville, PA

Published by Fulton Books 2021

All scriptures, unless otherwise stated, are taken from
the King James Version of the Holy Bible.

ISBN 978-1-63860-516-4 (paperback)
ISBN 978-1-63860-517-1 (digital)

Printed in the United States of America

To the memory of my late mother, Cynthia Marie Patten-Barfield. This is for her who always pushes me to strive to be better.

Contents

••◦❮◆❯◦••

Foreword

••◦)◆(◦••

As I began the journey of book writing, many questions resonated in my mind that hopefully will help you or someone you may know. How did I make it this far? What kind of journey have I really been on? How can my experiences help others in life? How much more can I gain on this journey? Is the time right for me to come forth with the sharing of my experiences?

We will take this journey together as I hopefully share with you that you too can find that right path in your spirit and natural man or woman to what you define as your successful way.

Preface

••◦)◆(◦••

To God be the glory for the inspiration to write this book, and many thanks to Him for allowing the Holy Spirit to guide my thoughts and bring back to my memory key events that I have experienced that will help others. I am truly humbled to know Him as a Father and His Son, Jesus Christ, as my Savior.

Many thanks to the love of my life of thirty-plus years, my wonderful wife, Linda Dorsey-Patten. You have been my number one fan and supporter in all that I have endeavored to do. You have shown me the way to true love which has helped remove the pains of my early scars of life. I am forever grateful for all that you have contributed and are still contributing to my life! Keep on believing in, praying for, and supporting me as I give my all to be about my father's business.

To my three sons and daughters-in-law, Aronte'(NaTasha), Jairus (Kimberly), and Zelik; and my grandchildren, Serenity, Harmony, Ayden, and Jalyn; my love for you helps propel the mission to provide inspirations and motivations that will catapult you to the next level.

A very special thanks to my late mother, Cynthia Marie Patten-Barfield, for being there as a motivator and number one mentor from my birth until her heavenly transition in 2016. I will forever cherish her memory, teachings, dedication, and passion. Her motto, "There's always room for improvement," remains constant with me. She will always be my hero as she persevered through some of life's toughest battles with unwavering faith in and commitment to God.

Special recognitions to my biological dad, Aaron Patten Sr. You taught me so many life-sustaining skills early in life. Even though you allowed me room to make my own choices, you were stern when it comes to making sure I was prepared to take care of myself. I got my mechanical and welding skills from your teachings—even my basics in cooking.

To my stepdad, Michael Barfield, thank you for exemplifying marriage vows in action. Thank you for taking care of Mom and showing how to walk through with your loved ones.

Thanks also to my spiritual parents, Bishop Stanley and co-pastor Brenda Searcy, for the many years of teaching and mentoring according to the Gospel of Jesus Christ. Without God putting you all in my life, none of this would have come to fruition. You continue to amaze me with pouring out God's freely given wisdom.

Many thanks to my grandparents, siblings, nieces, nephews, other relatives, teachers, and friends that have played major roles in shaping my life story. Thank you all for the support and wisdom. You all have contributed in significant ways to my growth into the person that I am today. My love for all of you that have played any role is immeasurable!

Introduction

•• ⟩◆⟨ ••

This book was written to encourage you who are dealing with the life challenges that I have faced. Hopefully, it will be an inspiration for you to keep pushing forth toward your destination. There is no greater desire than that I can make a difference in the lives of those that will choose to hear my story.

Chapter 1
Determinations

••◦)◆◦••

There are natural-born determinations in every individual. How we cultivate those determinations to full maturation are up to us. My purpose for writing this book is to share with you some valuable lessons that I have learned throughout the course of my life that I hope will be of help to you. As I allow my mind to reflect back over my life, I am thankful for the experiences that have taught me different lessons. Most of the lessons were good, but there were some which were not so good. However, all the life lessons I have learned have helped chart my course in life.

I challenge you to read page by page and chapter by chapter, as there are many experiences that I will share which may propel you through situations that are hindering you from gaining all that you need to reach the level of success that you desire. I encourage you to have those you care about to purchase their copies to share with individuals—young and mature—that may need some guidance with situations they have dealt with or are dealing with in life.

Currently, I hold a master mechanical contractor's license, a mortgage loan officer's license, a real estate salesperson's license, and a trainee appraiser' license. I am operating in positions in several of our family-owned firms. I have been in these capacities dating back as 2005. The journey started out from an idea formulated in the den of my current home after I have experienced two really disheartening failed business transactions. Getting these firms started and keeping them operational during one of the greatest depressions in United States history have in no way been easy tasks. But perseverance pays.

All glory goes to God for His favor in the midst of all the challenges. I will talk more about the business firms later in this book.

In order for you to really grasp where my life story to success is taking you, I must share my story from early childhood to now. In it, it is important for me to take you through the straight paths and crooked paths experiences. Are you ready for this harling journey?

Being born and raised in the small country town of Lorman, Mississippi, was rewarding and challenging in itself. I was the eldest of three siblings born to my parents. Our community's population at the time of my birth was probably less than a thousand. Many of the families that lived in Lorman at the time lived in extreme poverty. My household was not in the extreme category, but we were living in poverty. Many times, I can remember our neighbors coming by to borrow household goods to feed and care for their family. Some of my friends knew the family that would talk down about them, but my mom would always tell me not to look down or make fun of them. I really did not understand at the time why she instilled that in me.

My family and I made the best of what we had, which was not much. Thankfully, we were a creative bunch who did not mind sharing. We made basketball hoops, bikes, swings, stick horses even though we had plenty of live horses, and you name it. Boy, we were creative! We used that creativity for mostly positive things. Let me assure you that there was never a dull moment. Too much of this is missing in society today, thus creating a different breed of mindsets.

My mother's story of growing up shed so much light on why she taught me not to look down on those who do not have. My mother had to drop out of high school due to birthing me at a very young age. One year and two months later, she gave birth to her second child, Sharon Patten-Bradford. Mom later returned to school to get her GED. After working hard and receiving her diploma, she started attending at Alcorn State University. She told numerous stories of having to walk so far to catch rides to college, but she never gave up. How Mom maneuvered being a wife, mother, and a full-time student was beyond my comprehension. She finished her bachelor's degree in mathematics education just prior to giving birth to her third child, Sheriff Travis Patten.

My mother was eventually hired as math teacher at the Claiborne County School District. After securing employment, she continued her education until she had earned her master's in education. There was no stopping Mom from reaching a goal that she probably did not see at first. That is why I call her my hero. She was just determined to not let success escape her even while enduring every possible bit of opposition. If your mother is still alive, take time to honor her with all that is in you. It will help you find peace on your path to success.

Prior to my birth, my dad had graduated from high school and went to work full-time as a forklift operator at Parks Lumber Company in Port Gibson, Mississippi. He still had to carry out his duties on the family farm. Dad was an extremely hard worker then, and his work ethics continues still. He, just as I did, started out as a young parent who made many mistakes early but had to make amends and improve parenting skills. Due to Mom going to school and Dad working full-time and carrying out his duties on the family farm, my siblings and I spent a lot of time between our grandparents' homes.

On my mother's side of the family, my grandparents did not have much, but they contributed greatly to my upbringing. I learned to be contented with what I have, work hard to feed my family, to love each other unconditionally, and how to fish. All of this impacted my life just as having all the ingredients to making good cornbread. I told y'all that I am a country boy. I spent many of days at work with my grandmother, Viola "Sis" Reynolds. Not only was she my grandmother, but she was also our school's cook. She would make sure that I would eat and sit waiting quietly on her each day to finish up at work. Oh yes, I was quiet because that willow tree limb she had would burn my legs if she had to use it on me. On the week-end, my grandmother, my grandfather, James "Son" Reynolds, along with Aunt Te-Wee would take us fishing. They took so much time teaching me all the trades of fishing and using all of the day's catch. Moments like these I have cherished for a very long time.

Farming and logging were the biggest strides of my dad's family as we grew up mostly on my grandparents' farm. It was a 215-acre farm that I learned early on and had enough work to go around.

My granddad, Charlie "Pie" Patten, had worked hard at logging to purchase the property with cash. I often tell my wife about the lessons my grandfather taught me. My cousins and I had to learn every aspect of working on the farm; planting and harvesting crops, preserving the crops once they were harvested, raising swine, raising cattle/horses, and raising chickens to harvest their eggs. We lived off the production of the farm and sold goods to others for their well-being and ours. This instilled in me—a hardworking ethic that has followed me through life. My granddad would always allow us to learn the lessons of entrepreneurship.

Granddad was a great teacher and wise businessman. I can recall many trips that he would take us on to the cattle, hog, and horse sales at the Lorman Stockyard. He was so proud to show off his grandchildren; but when it comes to bidding on the livestock, he made sure that we pay close attention.

Little did I know at the time that his lessons would prove so valuable to me later in my adult life. Boy, do I wish that I had more than ten years to glean off of his teachings. I learned the true value of family and mentorship, and that success can be better gained by learning from the greatest of teachers.

My grandmother, Mary "Yemi" Patten, was a housewife, but she had the family business at heart. She was devoted to supporting my granddad in running all aspects of the farm. She made sure us grandchildren learned our manners and helped out around the house. Yemi was the enforcer in making sure that the family attended and participated in church. The only ones that were excused were the ones working with Pie. We pulled water from the cistern, chopped firewood, fed the animals, gathered eggs, salted the smokehouse meat, and many other chores. She taught the girls to cook, but we boys were not allowed in the kitchen. We just had our hands in the outside chores.

I can clearly remember my granddad's passing in 1982 in the Jefferson County Hospital. I recall our mother taking us to visit him at the Jefferson County Hospital. I recall our mother taking us to visit him a day or so before he passed away. Now that I look back at the visit, I believe that it was a moment not only to say goodbye, but for him to pass on his anointing in entrepreneurship to his grandchildren. This still took a gigantic toll on our family as he was the patriarch of our family—a man of great wisdom and full of authority. I can recall my grandmother, dad, and his siblings working to carry on the family business. They would even allow me to be in the room when they were counting the cash to make equipment purchases. I still did not get that this was part of my continuing education to become a successful entrepreneur. That was definitely a Proverbs 22:6 KJV, "Train up a child in the way he should go; and when he is old, he will not depart from it," moment. I believe that this counts in following the ways of the Lord and living a good life of doing what is right in other ways as well.

His passing also brought a change in the dynamics of the family business in the way that he was heavy on the cattle and horse operation, which had kept the stockyards in Lorman operational for many years; but the family was starting to slowly back out the part of the business.

Not long after his passing, was my grandmother waiting on a hot Mississippi day to march in with the choir to church that she took sick and never recovered to live a normal life. The second in the family command structure was now incapacitated. So what would our plan be to carry on the family business? This is what I consider my first opportunity—to learn how to deal with adversity and keep moving forward in a positive direction. I genuinely loved my grandparents and the time they invested in me as I spent time with them. It was hard to see my granddad pass away and watched my grandmother slowly lose her health.

The farm life even allowed me to learn to drive at a very young age, as most city children could not do because of license requirements. I was shown once or twice the basics of driving and soon after, released to learn to drive the tractor so I could grasp the skill of driving. I was later afforded the opportunity to transport my uncles; one who was elderly, and one who was handicap, that did not drive to their various destinations. As a young man, this was such a joy as driving was the "in" thing. My older cousins had enjoyed these opportunities, but they grew out of them for dating, sports activities, etc., so I was obliged to take over these duties.

As with most young men, I had my good and not so good experiences coming through the remainders of my childhood. Even as we
hear a lot about it during today's times, I had to deal with bullying,
peer pressure, and being looked down for not having a whole lot or
fitting in with the crowd. These could have left life scars that could
have caused me to turn, permanently, to the wrong things to bring
me out of the hurt from them. But with the correct guidance and
the grace of God, I was able to get through them lightly scarred,
and now with the ability to help others master overcoming the same
experiences. It is a heavy burden for a young person to bare so much
on their own, so seek help if you need it. I am a living testimony that
there are times that it helps to be helped.

Chapter 2
Observing and Learning

••◦◦

Moving through my teenage years, by observing and learning what I could from my parents, grandparents, aunts, uncles, cousins, teachers, mentors, and friends, proved helpful in where I am today in life as a middle-aged African American male living in the south. This came with many trials and great tests. I can recall my time in the Boy Scouts—learning teamwork and survival in the midst of difficulty. Our scoutmaster was a white male, but our troop was made up of all Black males. He had a heart of pure gold, and he made sure that we had what it took to thrive in a world as it was at that time. He played a large role in shaping me not to hate for being wronged. He would teach us the life of being scouts, and he gave us opportunities in the 1980s to interact with other troops of all races. This meant a lot as I look back now and reflect on of the good and really bad experiences that I had while being a scout.

The scouting opportunities were many, but I will only share a couple of them. I had the opportunity to visit Washington, DC, early on via a scout trip. This was a trip that I will always remember. We toured the interior of the White House, the US Mint, a host of national monuments, and many other significant national treasures. We did have a hiccup for not following our going to bed early instructions while on the trip. As I said earlier in this book, this was not an expectation for a small country boy out of Lorman, Mississippi. So much was learned on this trip and I still appreciate our leaders for giving me the opportunity to go.

My next treasured Boy Scout trip was when we had a small older group travel to the North Carolina mountains on a hiking trip. On the night of our arrival, us, troops were given strict instructions on getting something to eat and return to our hotel rooms immediately afterward. Of course, being young, we just could not do that. We had to eat and go play pool at a local pool hall that we had spotted. We had fun at first, but the night ended with an unforgettable experience.

We played our first few games and were getting ready to start another game when we discovered that we were surrounded by all white men with fire in their eyes. Boy, I was a scared young man! The men surrounded us and gave us the story of the last African American that had visited the community, and how he had been hung from the tree across the street from the pool hall. This shook me to the very core and has remained in my mind for various reasons. There was a high cost to pay for being disobedient and I did learn that the hard way.

Needless to say, we ran full speed back to the hotel, and ended up spending the night on the floor in the hotel rooms with the scout leaders. They were glad that we were safe, but they surely gave us the "I told you so" speech when we had finished our hiking trip and were headed back to Mississippi. As I have mentioned, this was a life lesson that helps me deal with what we are seeing and happening in the world today.

As I entered into my mid teenage years of life, another set of curve balls came my way. A whole lot more of family sickness, death, and other turmoil. My parents' marriage would not endure this for various reasons that I will not disclose in this book. Instead, this will be a reflection on me as to how I had endured this devastating event and stayed the course toward success. My parents went on to get a divorce when I was fifteen years old as way too many people can relate to. This set me on a course for my first failure in my young life.

My grades in school dropped tremendously, and my attitude shifted for the worse. I lived with my mother for a short time, but she had such strict rules that I rebelled against them and chose to go live with my dad. This gave me the opportunity to enjoy my freedom as I could go and come as I pleased. It also gave me the opportunity to hang with crowds who would pursue trouble at times that set me on a course for potential major consequences.

By all means, this is not a tell-it-all book, so I will only give the key factors of trouble that could have gotten me locked in prison and definitely off of the success path that I was destined for. This will help some young person without a doubt. I got in with groups that indulged in illegal street racing, dealing without a pharmacist's license, and picking up things without properly purchasing them. Some of these guys were hardcore, and something in me would say that I did not fit in.

Do not look down on me, but hear me out as this is where getting off course which can steer you. That success that was in me from birth "Let us make man in our image, after our likeness" (Genesis 1:26) was slowly fading away, and the really bad thing is that I could not see it as a young naïve teenager. I just could not phantom that I was not on the right path. All that I could see was fun, fast money, and freedom. Whew, I was wrong about this whole concept!

My mother had done all that she could to keep me on track even though I was not living with her. She knew that I had the success gene in my DNA and that failure was not an option. She would make sure that I stayed attending church and stayed active in the Boy Scouts. With all of the activities between these two entities, she was sure that I would bounce back from their divorce and other issues that I had faced.

Our church at the time was very traditional so it did not have extracurricular activities to keep me well occupied outside church times. We would have services only twice a month, but it did keep me out of the streets for those times. This was no excuse for my being mischievous outside church times.

The Boy Scouts were more accommodating as I was able to compete with my peers, and again, learn some valuable lessons for my life's journey. My hat is off again to my scoutmaster for dedicating so much time to our all Black scout troop. It really helped most of us see the best in each other. He trained me so many life skills that are so valuable even today. The troop only missed one thing that I really wanted to learn and that was how to swim. That lake in Hazlehurst, Mississippi, was just too muddy for me to stick out the lessons. Again, my scout leaders were such great inspirations in a time when my young life was really spiraling in the wrong direction.

I hung out with quite a few family members and close friends on a regular basis. Though I enjoyed the time with them, my eyes were becoming opened. There were a few things that ignited a fire in me that I knew that the path that I had drifted to was not the one for me. I watched some of those same family members and friends began being incarcerated; two others died as teenagers, and some of them became addicted to drugs.

Now, I was not immune to the activities around me. "Bad company corrupts good character" (1 Corinthians 15:33). At seventeen, I received a free ride to the Claiborne County Jail for illegal drag racing. I ended up with a whole bunch of traffic violations. It could have been a much worse ending. Thank God, Dad made it there before I was processed and locked in a cell! I believe that I really would have totally freaked out! Oh yeah, that put a sense of urgency on me to make a positive change! Believe me, you can have some wake up calls in life that gets your full attention.

Chapter 3
Time for a Change

●●·❯◆❮·●●

My change would start with me changing high schools at the beginning of my eleventh-grade year. My wife, Linda, played the biggest role in that change and the change of my life to get me back on track. We had talked on the phone a few years before this time via mutual friends, but we lost contact. This opportunity came again, and this time we exchanged phone numbers and kept in contact. I really thank God for that! This part of my life was such an impactful change, so pay close attention.

As we talked across the phone during this time prior to my junior year of high school, we fell in love without ever seeing each other. That opportunity did not come until the senior class before her graduation. I attended that graduation ceremony to see a friend graduate. Man, I was happy, impressed, and relieved! The beauty matched everything from our hearts that had been shared over many phone calls that we had experienced.

Needless to say, I had my dad transfer me from Jefferson County to Claiborne County High School to pursue our opportunity to date and spend time with Linda. This really contributed me getting back on track. There were some bumps in the road, but not to the extent of what I had experienced in the recent years.

I was compelled to move forward and I knew that I needed to change my environment, so I enlisted in the military. I also knew that I wanted to marry Linda. We were smart enough to know that her parents (Ida and John Bridgeman and John Campbell) nor my parents were going to go for that, so we came up with a plan. We decided that Linda would get pregnant. Our plan worked, and we were married in July after her graduation. I had one more year to go, so I had to dig in. I asked my dad to allow me to return to my previous school for my senior year, but he put his foot down and made me stay put. Linda was also in agreement with him. In September 1991, I left my wife and son, Aronte', to head off to train to become an airman in the US air force.

Disclaimer: I would not recommend this to teenagers because the outcome may not be as blessed as mine.

My journey into the air force was an experience of a lifetime and helped save me from some major trouble that others around me found themselves in soon after I left for basic training. Man, God had His hand on me at the right time! I went through basic training, both mentally and physically with ease. I really missed my family during training, but I learned how to embrace new friendships and a brotherhood among the airmen that I trained with. The greatest thing about it was race or creed did not matter for you to bond with others as you just knew you had to have each other's backs. I had multiple friends that failed the obstacle course needed for graduation on the first try. I did not look down on them because of their failures. I, along with others, stepped up and coached them on how to master the course. They were overjoyed and appreciative for the help and coaching. This is what I feel that helps you find success. As I finished my training, my family came to see me graduate and it brought me so much joy in seeing that so many cared! All of us like to feel loved, and that is a big factor in becoming successful.

Upon completing basic training in San Antonio, Texas, I was transferred to Wichita Falls, Texas, for training on my assigned field of study which was heating, ventilation, air conditioning, and refrigeration. I was excited as I was already very mechanically inclined from learning from my dad how to work on any and everything. Also, the transfer allowed Linda and Aronte' to actually come live with me while I completed my training. This was an extremely happy time for our young family. We made the best out of our short stay in Wichita Falls, and we made some short-term friends just to helps us past the time. We even sharpened our skills in learning how to live on our own as we had lived with my dad for our first year of marriage.

We really bonded as a family that was now living on our own. The training carried me into a work field that followed me throughout my air force career and is still contributing to my success story.

My air force career after training took me to my permanent workstation at Holloman Air Force Base in New Mexico. Nowhere on my list of preferred base assignments was this place. The desert and dry heat proved to be a bit much for this high humidity young man out of Mississippi. Even now, as I reflect back, the leadership at work could have been much better for the proper grooming and treating of all young men. I had stepped into an environment far from home and with all new faces. How was this going to contribute to where I am now? Needless to say, I worked hard and learned as much as I could—given the circumstances. Everything was different than what I had experienced at the bases in Texas. There were airman all over the place working and living freely. I actually could work in the area that I had trained in. This was a good feeling.

At the same time, I was having to improve on my husband and father skills. I must admit that I did not do a good job in this area early on. I had brought too much baggage with me from the trauma that I had experienced as a child. Linda got to see the very worst side of me at times, and I am so sorrowful for that. She just endured and prayed that I would get better. I thought for sure that she would throw in the towel on our marriage, but she held in there. We are both glad that she did. If you are married and really want to find success, always include your spouse in your vision. It will make life a whole lot better for you. Take it from me, I know that it works. We also had the opportunity to make lifelong friendships with couples while at Holloman Air Force Base that we still stay in contact with. Their marriages were good examples for us as they were strong, and that truly helped us.

The actual job of being an airman proved to be both good and bad as I may have said early on. The work was very hectic at times, both from the air conditioning work and military trainings. I can recall my first field training exercise. We had to simulate war time activities. I had no clue what to do in parts of the field exercises, so I stuck out like a sore thumb! One superior finally pulled me to the side and walked me through what to do, and after that, others started to step up and help me learn the ropes. That is what I believed which kicked off the teamwork concept among us airmen that helped us keep our sanity at the time. The air conditioning work side of things proved to provide a strong learning curve to maneuver through. I just had to jump in where I could, and learn from those that actually taught you how to work on the various systems. For the most part, the majority of the guys did not mind teaching you as long as you did not exceed knowing what they knew. It was competition with restrictions. The main boss came off as one that made sure you knew that he was the boss, but he had a lot of work knowledge and knowledge of where everything was on the base. As I reflect back, he really had a problem with airmen of color. He would subject me and others to degrading conversations and clearly, he treated us differently. He would constantly tell us that the blacks and Mexicans were to be the workers not the supervisors. Some of the things that he said are just too ugly to share in this book. Isn't it ironic that I can still remember the conversations with him some twenty-five-plus years later? That is because the scars remain, but I do not let them stop me from writing my success story in life. Although the enemy has assigned people to you with the task of trying to deter you from your purpose, put you down, and degrade you, remember that God has a plan for you that no one can stop. I encourage you to press through the pain of those around you, belittling you. Your victory and success are on the other side. Just remember, you are God's creation.

You can get caught up in foolishness like that and it will stunt your growth, so address what you need to and move on. I compel you to move forward knowing that regardless of what you are going through, God has a bigger plan and purpose for your life. Jeremiah 29:11 states, "For I know the thoughts that I think toward you, saith the Lord, thoughts of peace, and not of evil, to give you an expected end." Let it be the best in driving you to be a better you. I am hopeful that my not speaking up back then did not subject too many more airmen to have to endure undue criticism and disparaging experiences.

Midway through my being stationed at Holloman, I was sent on a temporary duty assignment to Homestead Air Force Base in Homestead, Florida. This assignment was to serve in relief of Hurricane Andrew which had devastated south Florida. This was an experience that impacted my heart and body. We had to clean up on the air force base, as well as feed those in the community that had lost everything. I had not ever seen so much destruction in a community, nor had I seen so many people that did not have food from day to day. Our feeding lines were as long as the eye could see, and they included many children. This left a soft spot in my heart to understand what my mother had taught me about caring for those who were misfortunate.

As I finished up my third year at Holloman, I had the intentions of extending my time in the air force and being transferred to a base overseas for my next assignment. The orders were ready, but an issue with taking my family with me caused this transfer not to come to fruition. I ended up not accepting the orders with the plan to get out of the air force at the end of my fourth year of active duty.

The very civilian boss that had talked down and degraded the minorities and religious airman was disappointed to hear that I was not going to reenlist for four more years. His behavior still irks me, but it has not hindered me from being focused on the mission at hand. It appears that he felt that I was one of the better airmen that had worked for him. He hosted a shop party for my going away and gave me plaques and other parting gifts. Some I have kept for a remembrance of my time there. Battered and bruised mentally and physically, my time on active military duty had come to an end.

Chapter 4

••◦)◆(◦••

As I transitioned out of Holloman Air Force Base in the mid-1990s, my hopes were to land a job in Atlanta, Georgia. There was plenty of hype about the 1996 Olympics coming there, so I had convinced my wife that this would be a good destination for our family after my military service time. I had made contact with potential employers who seemed eager to consider me for employment in the heating and air conditioning field. Also, we had searched for housing which at the time were apartments for rent. Surprisingly, there were a lot of options available at the time.

What we thought was our game plan for the future never came to fruition. That was just not in the path of success that we were destined to be on. We made a big change on our plans. We decided to return to Mississippi to be close to our families. This set us on a course that has been very promising and rewarding. I immediately found employment with a nationally known automotive repair shop with the understanding that I would be doing automotive air conditioning and other minor repairs. Let me tell you, this was definitely not my "cup of tea!" I had to do the same repairs as the other mechanics, and it was six-day workweeks. It was necessary at the time but some dirty work.

It pays to have God place people in your life. He gave me my help mate that has always believed in me. Linda and I did not believe that what I was doing was what I was meant to do. About two months of working at the automotive repair shop, Linda found out that both of the local hospitals posted job announcements for a heating, ventilation, air conditioning, and refrigeration technician. I had her pickup applications from both as I was working and could not get by to pick them up.

I applied at both hospitals, but only got a call from one of them. I was interviewed by the largest of the two. I thought that the interview had gone okay, but I could not really tell if I had gotten the job. I did not hear back for weeks, so I called just to check the status of my application. I was offered the job, but the pay rate that I requested was turned down. I took the lower amount not knowing that I could have stood firm and probably have gotten the amount that I had requested. So much in hindsight did I learn through the whole hiring experience.

To truly be successful, I just believe that the most challenging experiences can bring the best out of you. You are not operating just on education; you are using every option, experience, and the intellect of our King of kings to push you past the challenges. "God is our refuge and strength, an ever present help in the times of trouble" (Psalm 46:1). That was my motivation early on as I was starting the job and gaining more valuable experience at the hospital. Man, this was a scary but rewarding time of my life!

As I started out in heating, ventilation, air conditioning, and refrigeration work at the hospital, I quickly found out that there were more advanced systems that I did not have the necessary experience to work on. This challenged me more to learn by studying my books from earlier training and leaning on an electrician / air conditioning technician that had been working there for many years. He did not appear to be receptive at all to me at the time. He challenged my knowledge on my first tour of the kitchen equipment and systems that I would be responsible for working on. Some of the tenured staff members that worked in the kitchen came to my rescue and let him know that he needed to give me a chance to learn the systems and that he needed to help me with the learning process. That felt good to have them come to my rescue! Again, I was the newbie on the block. This would set the course for a twelve-year rewarding journey while working at the hospital.

My first year or so was a task, to say the least. I had so much to learn and so many work areas and coworkers to get to know. The work-related learning got easier over time as I had unexpected people step up to the plate to help where they could. I gleaned as much as

I could from everyone no matter what their jobs were. I was using my "sponge effect" to just soak up the knowledge of every process, procedure, and all else. I did not know at the time that my learning would prove so valuable in such a quick manner.

My boss was one that would push you sometimes to the max and sometimes to the point of nerve wrecking, but now I know that it was for the best of the hospital. He saw something in me that I did not see in myself. He personally taught me a lot about hospital construction and blueprint reading. He challenged me to learn systems outside the air conditioning realm. While going through the process, I was being told by my peers that I needed to ask for more money. I'm glad that I did not ask at the time as my boss really poured some key knowledge into my life, and he gave me chances to learn and lead.

Later on, I did begin to think that I deserved more money as my work assignments were consistently going beyond my job description. As time went on, I did more and more additional work duties including a lot of compliance paperwork for the hospital accreditation group. This stirred me to believe that I should be paid more. Inside, I wanted to believe that my coworkers had been correct, but I still did not approach my boss about being compensated extra. I just stayed the course until my job evaluation time came around. I negotiated hard at evaluation time, and my boss ended up getting me up to what I had initially asked for before starting the job.

Two years on the job, I joined a spirit-filled ministry which I will talk about its impact on my life. Being under the ministry changed the course of the remainder of my employment at the hospital and has continued to help hone my entrepreneur skills. I also enrolled in college seeking a degree in business administration; took on a part-time job at an apartment complex; started performing air conditioning repair work as an independent contractor, all while being actively involved in so many other things. This was another challenging time as Linda had enrolled in college and was working part-time. Successful direction will lead you to and through multiple challenges.

Shortly afterward, I found out that a technical college in the neighboring state of Louisiana was searching for a HVAC/R instructor. I applied because I had heard that the position paid a considerable amount of money. This amount was well above what I was getting paid at the hospital, and the work environment was much more relaxed.

My interview for the instructor's job went exceptionally well. Needless to say, I was offered the position with the higher salary. I so badly wanted to accept it as I thought that it was my destiny. Know this, more money is not always and indicator of being successful.

I met with my boss at the hospital to let him know that I had interviewed and was offered a position to teach heating, ventilation, air conditioning, and refrigeration. At first, he was wishing me well with the new job and asking how much notice I would be giving to allow him time to hire my replacement. He was the type that you really could not read what he was thinking so I was preparing myself mentally for the new job.

The talkative coworkers were in disbelief that I had submitted my resignation. They were also very quick to point out that when you submit a resignation in our department, you would be let go that day that you turned it in. This did not happen to me. It was just the opposite of the way that they had told me past experiences had gone on with others. Instead, my boss inquired about what it would take for me to stay.

Chapter 5

•• ❭◆❬ ••

A door had opened in a two-year time frame and that door was a big opening. "I know your works. See I set before you an open door, and no one can shut it" (Revelation 3:8). I gave him the salary number that the school had offered and made it clear that it would take that amount for me to stay at the hospital. He informed me that in my current position, the salary amount was too high to match, so a new position would have to be created with more job duties. Low and behold, I had already been performing the duties, but had not been getting compensated for the work. When the job was posted, only a few of us applied.

My coworkers that applied knew that I had been performing the duties and that the position was geared toward me. You must be willing to sacrifice a little to get to that success that you are striving for.

I applied and was awarded the new position, so I did the best thing for me, and hopefully, the hospital by staying. My learning increased over into learning the management side of the department. My boss stretched and challenged me to the max in a non-spiteful manner. He was grooming me for my future. Only one coworker became bitter over my promotion, but he was able to move on as he saw how effective I was in the position and around the hospital. I worked my heart out and gained so many new skills, friends, and respect while working. Many of the people that I worked with became lifelong friends to me. They are still on my mind, and I pray for them as often as I can. That is a part of being successfully driven. My initial trainer even took on a liking to me and would often tell me how good of a job that I was doing. He challenged me to get my state mechanical license, and I obliged.

As I continued to grow in my new position, my boss continued to put more assignments on my lists. This did not distract me from thriving to do my job because my support system was strong. To my surprise, my boss was taking a position at another hospital in another city. He had been preparing me all along, but I had no clue. He informed me that he was leaving. He also informed me that he recommended me to the CEO and promote me to the director's position. Never having any interaction with the CEO, I was shaking on my boots because I had no idea what he thought about me. Would he have confidence in my ability to oversee a department of seventeen employees along with all the other duties of being the department's director? He did not interview me, nor did he interview anyone else for the position. The CEO put the "interim" title on the position and put me in it with the biggest pay raise that I could have imagined! I was shocked and relieved all at the same time, and I thought it was my road to success. My plan would be to ride it out until retirement. Well, it was not!

I had many big surprises heading my way. The CEO was impressed with my work ethics, and the way I was running the department. He afforded me the opportunity to expand my knowledge by sending me to visit more advanced hospitals. One of the hospitals was one he had managed in El Paso, Texas. This hospital was a state-of-the-art hospital that inspired many ideas which I could take back to my hospital.

Our hospital did not have the funds like the other hospitals for all the ideas I had. The CEO did take my advice on pushing for with setting up the helipad. His idea was to put it on the roof, but I had another idea. To my delight, the CEO went with my idea. The helipad has been a tremendous asset to our community that I am proud to have been a part of getting in place.

I worked at the hospital for a total of twelve years. By that time, I had grown in knowing God through the powerful teachings I had received at my church. Not only was I learning the word of God, but I was also actually participating in performing the principals of the word. I will not share everything in case my pastors write a book in the future, sharing the glorious journey that God took the ministry on. I will say we worked for the better of the total man (body, soul, and spirit).

One thing that I can say which contributed to my success is not shying away from working in all aspects of the ministry. I have worn many hats and performed many duties as assigned. I believe in my heart that this has pleased God and He's blessed me in other areas of my life because of my sincere commitment to His ministry. You do this not in a manipulative way but in a pure of heart way, and I believe God's Favor will follow you on your road to success.

During the time of my transitioning from working at the hospital, I had been actively working on construction projects for the church. We had physically renovated every aspect of our first sanctuary. I learned a ton about aspects of construction that I did not have to do in the past while working on the first sanctuary. By the time that we finished renovating the first sanctuary, it was time to start the planning for the new sanctuary that had to be constructed.

We went through many steps and phases to prepare for this project. All the while God was blessing the growth of our family businesses. I worked on the teams to prepare the packets for the financing to the team that reviewed the blueprints for construction. The groundbreaking took place during the same year that we were able to break ground on our home. Let me tell you that I gained so much knowledge from being a part of both projects. This has contributed so much to my growth and development, and it definitely is continuing to expand my success story.

Chapter 6
Staying the Course

••◦)◦◆◦(◦••

Meanwhile, the new administration at the hospital had come in and were making overall drastic changes. In my opinion, these changes were made without a clear knowledge and vision of what they were doing. Seeing the direction, the hospital was going in, placed me in an uncomfortable position. My pastor had prophesized to me some years prior to this happening. God had plans for me to do more to help the community and the underserved. He made it clear that when the time comes for me to move, things would become extremely uncomfortable at the hospital. That time came over the course of some years, and so did the opportunity to really get into position to be able to help many families over the southwest part of the United States.

In 2002, Linda and I were treated unfairly on a mortgage loan application by a local bank. We had completed an application to purchase land and to construct a home. The banker made no effort to call or update us on the status of our application, so I made contact with that banker. Shockingly, I was informed that we could purchase an existing home, but we could not purchase land and build a home. I did not understand the ruling. We had excellent credit, money saved, and official house plans to build, so what was the reason for the denial? Thankfully, one of the contractors we had contacted to build our home recommended another bank. Following his advice, we completed an application at that bank. We were approved without any problems whatsoever.

The most disturbing part about the whole home financing with the first bank is that my assistant and their spouse applied shortly after our terrible experience with the same bank. They were approved for a home construction loan with no problem at all. At the time, I could not digest what had gone wrong with the experience with the first bank. They obviously had some issues that needed addressing.

Toward the end of my tenure at the hospital, we had another bad experience with a mortgage transaction. This time, a mortgage refinance transaction had gone wrong. A bank had intentions of taking advantage of us with inflated fees and a risky loan. Little did I know that this area would be my calling. Although I did not have any experience in mortgage lending or anything related to it, I knew I did not want anyone else to experience what Linda and I had experience with that bank and that transaction. Remember, my career was in buildings and grounds maintenance, and I put all my energy and efforts in perfecting my knowledge, skills, and techniques into it. After all, I thought I was going to retire doing that. That would not be the case!

By 2005, the internet craze was moving forward, so I found a mortgage loan officer class online and decided to take the course. I also found a class and company that would work with us to do credit repair since this was a hot topic in our community. I went through the courses and convinced my sister, who is an RN to do the same. Both of us took the class and earned our licenses.

Chapter 7
Decisions

••>◆<••

Now, we had to decide who was going to leave their job and start our business. With the guidance of the Lord and a spirit-filled pastor pushing us along the way, we started the process of starting our business in the den of our home. This was the best thing we could have done.

After diligently searching for office space to rent, we were unable to locate one. However, we did find a building that had a for sale or rent sign in the window. When we contacted the owner, we were told that we could only buy the building and for us to make an offer. We saw the hefty price on the building and questioned ourselves whether we should buy a building for an unproven business. After praying about it, we made an offer on the building that was less than half of the asking price. She accepted the offer without hesitation! Now, not only was my confidence being built, but our entire family was inspired.

My sister and one other person started up the business at our new location. I only worked at the business after my hours of working at the hospital. Linda and I helped with the books and marketing. We had a lot to learn in an area where neither one of us had experience. There was not anyone willing to help us learn the business, but God, our pastor, family, and some of our church family were with us.

We were able to open the doors to our business in August, 2005. Immediately afterward, here comes Hurricanes Katrina and Rita to shut us down for days at a time. However, we bounced back and got going. If you want success, you must earn it by working. Do not expect it to be given to you.

In 2007, I officially resigned from the hospital and joined the team at the mortgage office full time. Although we have had our struggles, we have stayed the course. Many appalling and unpleasant experiences and threats came our way. There were so many experiences that I will have to share them in another book because the purpose of this book is to provide you with valuable information that I hope will help you stay the course for your success.

As I stated earlier, no one came beating down the doors to offer advice on how to grow our business. We had to seek every avenue possible to learn what to do on our own. Whenever the opportunity arose for us to learn and grow, we took it, and it has paid off over the years.

Express Tax Finance Center was our initial business. We prepared taxes, assisted in credit restoration, and earned the trust of loyal customers by treating them with respect and dignity. However, we did not stop there.

Our business path and the negative experience Linda and I experienced, led us into the mortgage business. We knew we had to change our business name and wanted it to reflect what we wanted to be known for. After all, we were no longer just doing taxes. That was when Integrity Mortgage Center, LLC was birthed. The name was significant because our goal was to let our customers and clients know in our name and action that we would provide an honest service. Many individuals in our mortgage classes would express that they were in the business for the money, but it always meant more to us to provide families with decent homes than to see how big the commission checks were. It has shown over the years that the true heart in the business would make it and stand the tests of time. Our state, Mississippi, had over one thousand instate mortgage brokers, but now there are less than twenty-five.

I am not trying to make it sound easy on what we have been afforded to be able to do because it was difficult to get started. At times, I thought that it was time to get out of the business. However, God kept blessing us, so we decided to enter the real estate business.

Entering the real estate business was life changing. Once news spread that we had opened Integrity Realty, LLP, we were blatantly threatened that we would be "black balled and put out of business."

We had people slander our names and try to steer customers away from doing business with us. Some people laughed in our faces as if they were true friends but talked about us behind our backs. These things were painful and discouraging at times, but we continued walking the path God had allowed us to walk. Success, in any capacity, can be difficult to achieve, but with God's help, we persevered.

Over the course of our family's years in business, God has truly blessed us to be a blessing to many families that otherwise may have experienced what I had personally experienced in the pursuit of mortgage loans. Additionally, He has allowed us to open home construction and renovations companies along with a hardware store. It was definitely because of God's grace that our businesses have been established and able to thrive in our community because there have been plenty of competition.

It is now 2021, and I have been blessed to continue serving in multiple capacities, not just in the business arena. I am still active in ministry at church and outside church. One of my favorite duties at the ministry is being a delivery driver for the food pantry. Also, I am active with the local Children's Advocacy Board where I am honored to serve as term as board president. I have previously served on other boards, but this one is more of a God-driven one. There are many underserved and abused children that benefit from the services covered from this commitment.

Chapter 8
It's Your Time

●●◦❯◆❮◦●●

Now you have read this much and may not have a clear picture of how I went about "Finding the Right Direction for Success in Life." You may find yourself wondering how you will find yours. This will come with you defining what will bring success in your life. I cannot define your success because I have no idea as to what you would like to achieve. However, I can tell you mine this far.

As is the case with many youngsters, I wanted money to buy things and stuff but not necessarily to be rich. This is what I can recall while growing up. I thought for sure that if I had money to buy race cars, farm animals and farm equipment that I would definitely be successful. That is what growing up a little country boy can do for you. You really do not get the full scope of what is available to you.

As I have lived my life, I know that my success story has not been about the money that I have made. It has not been about the places I have visited or the vehicles I have owned. Nor has it been about the homes I have purchased. My right direction for success in life has been finding the true and living God and doing His will. His will has been about doing for others according to His word and not being focused on my wants. That to me is the ultimate feeling of being successful. My treasures are being planted for a time after this life even though I am living a good life here on earth.

I feel that His will was for me to get under a true Bible-based ministry back in 1997, and to continue doing His work as I have learned His word through the many years of teachings by my pastor and others along with studying the word for myself. The ministry has really impacted me both in the word of God and the enhancement of my entrepreneur skills. Back at a time, I was reeling at a crossroad in my life. It was highly like that not one of my businesses would be where they are today without keeping God first in all that I set out to do.

As you read my story, my life was tough starting out and there were stories that I did not put in this book because they were so despicable. In addition, I did not want to expose the people that brought these acts against me. You see, these were not just people I dealt with in the military or in business, they included family members and so-called friends as well. I have forgiven them and moved on because I learned many years ago that it could hinder my growth in God and life. My focus is to serve people in an honest way and afford them the opportunities that I was denied at some point in my adult life. It is the greatest joy to see a family purchase a home. Regardless as to whether I am representing them as their loan officer or real estate agent, joy bursts in my heart. It is more of a good feeling to see them than anything else.

It also does me good to see balances brought to parts of communities that are normally overlooked. Why not afford families access to affordable homes? Why not teach families how important it is to manage their credit or household finances? Why not educate young people on the importance of getting an education and working instead of hanging out? Why not use my social media platforms to promote the word of God?

Of course, in operating businesses, money is made, and I have to take care of my responsibilities to my family. The key is that I do not focus on the money because it can get me off my right path. I focus on the needs of the many clients that I serve. It is my feeling of success on this journey that I am now on.

Everything that has elevated me has come via the teachings and adhering to the word of God! There are no "ifs, ands, or buts" about it. This is whole heartedly what I know has gotten me heading in the right direct for success in life!

For you, your direction may be totally different from mine. You may see that making big money is your focus, which is okay for you if it does not cause you to lose your soul. My challenge to you is not let the hindrance that you may face get you heading in the wrong direction or even have you give up. There were many obstacles that I faced that could have changed my entire outlook in life, but I overcame them by God's generous grace. You can do the same and stay at the course of finding your right direction for success in your life.

If you are faced with racism, hate or being put down, you need not let it get you off your mission. Persevere and stay the course that is set before you. Falling to the pressure of one of these can stunt your growth or possibly cause you to take the direction of trouble or failure. I had many opportunities to take the wrong direction but as I stated early on, I did not.

Even let downs by family or friends can be detrimental to you, so walk carefully as you endure what they try to throw your way. You know within you that you are better than what the naysayers are saying about you, right? Your success is what you perceive it to be before it comes to pass. Before you create your direction, you research it to make sure that it will be an enjoyable one that you will stick with. If you are not happy on your mission, you just might not stay with it. Do your due diligence so you will not have to depend on others to hold your hand.

My hope is that you reach every goal on your path that you aim for. Keep hope living in you to the fullest and stay moving in the right direction. Nothing can stop you from reaching your success but you. Do not receive anything that will discourage you from staying the course for the entire time. You do have the power to do that so be encouraged!

I hope that this book has inspired you to seek God first in all things; to dream, to not let any circumstance, injustice or anyone hinder you. These items did not come to me overnight, so it is likely that you will not achieve them over night. No worries as that is surely okay. Work hard and get your goals set to find the right direction for your success in life!

About the Author

•••)◆(•••

A aron Patten Jr. is an intelligent, inspirational, courageous, creative individual who possesses a gentle spirit. After serving his country as a member of the United States Air Force, he has journeyed into various job fields and business arenas. He is a man who has overcome the hurt, pain, and disappointments of his past to lead a victorious life.

With the leading of the Lord and support of his family and pastor, Aaron walked away from being the first Black department manager of the maintenance department at a regional hospital to start his own business. The birth of that business has now grown to multiple businesses. Aaron has made it a priority to help others achieve their goals and dreams through his various businesses.

Aaron interest to write, grew as he saw his wife and late mother author books to encourage others in their lines of duty. He has worked tirelessly over the last few years to complete his first manuscript.

Aaron has been married to his high school sweetheart for thirty years. He is the proud father of three sons, honored father-in-law of two daughters-in-law, and the doting grandfather of four grandchildren. Aaron resides with his family in Natchez, Mississippi.

CPSIA information can be obtained
at www.ICGtesting.com
Printed in the USA
LVHW100555050422
715317LV00001B/142